Laura Ellis'

Shadow Dancer

Laura C. Ellis, Ph.D.

PublishAmerica
Baltimore

© 2006 by Laura C. Ellis, Ph.D.
All rights reserved. No part of this book may be reproduced, stored in a retrieval system or transmitted in any form or by any means without the prior written permission of the publishers, except by a reviewer who may quote brief passages in a review to be printed in a newspaper, magazine or journal.

First printing

At the specific preference of the author, PublishAmerica allowed this work to remain exactly as the author intended, verbatim, without editorial input.

ISBN: 1-4241-5082-5
PUBLISHED BY PUBLISHAMERICA, LLLP
www.publishamerica.com
Baltimore

Printed in the United States of America

Dedication

I dedicate this book to all who have helped me in life and paradoxically to the hardships that have inspired many of my poems. I am grateful for the love of my husband Tres, and my two beautiful German Shepherds, Woody and Rusty. Also to my family and friends.

In particular, I thank the Powers that be, for the gift of poetry and art that I have been so graciously blessed with.

Acknowledgement

I wish to thank R.W. Kisner for his help with this book, and Tres Ellis, my husband, for all of his support, and to my family, Michael and Ann Judd, Sarah Phelps, Clare Moore, Norris Fergeson, George Judd and Michael Judd, Jr.

I also thank Sue Pelzer Ph.D. for her encouragement throughout my life.

Finally I thank my readers for choosing to read my work.

Contents

The Survivor 9
My Favorite Thing 10
Don't Go There 11
The New Way 12
Life 13
The Horse 14
Questions 16
Time Waits for None 17
I Am a Tree 18
The Songs of Reality 20
The Present 21
The Mission 22
The Migration 23
An Inquiry 24
The Book 25
Love and Lost 26
To All Of My Friends Here 27
The Spirit That Got Remembered 28
Shall I? 29
The Trees and the Forest 31
Where and Why 32
Travel to the Stars 33
Will the Forest Survive? 34
Loss of Innocence 35
Lost at Sea 36
Human Wrongs 38
Who am I? 39
The Forest Fire 40

Greed	41
The Sun and the Sand	42
The Past	43
Wrong	45
The Lost	47
Another Storm Story	48
The Other Storm	49
Time	50
The Children	51
Nature's Wrath	52
Hidden	54
Island of Mine	55
The Tree	56
War Part 1	57
War 2	58
War 3	59
Dragons	60
The Candle	62
The Loss	63
Firefly	64
The Star	65
Leaves	66
Life and Death	67
Alaska	68
Sailor's Saga—Part One	69
The Raging Storm—Part Two	72
The Sailor Saga—Part Three	74
The Sailors Saga—Part Four	77
Ongoing Sea Saga—Part Five	79
The Children's Plight—Part Six	81

The Survivor

Walking along the rail of the bridge
She looks out and sees the mountain ridge
It is too beautiful to lose she knows it now
She asks herself in a place of such beauty…how?

Nature is her saving grace
In this materialistically ideological place
To avoid the cement and hard concrete
Without nature, life is simply incomplete

So down from the ledge she steps down and ponders
On the billions of stars in the dark sky she wanders
Wondering as always why why why
But the answer teasingly evades her…. sigh

She looks out at the tiny lights in the sky
White snow flakes twinkling up so very high
They are the stars of her whole existence
As the earth spins her along without any resistance

My Favorite Thing

I can smell the rain coming closer
The clouds swirl like a roller coaster
I can't wait for the storm to hit
As the sky grows purple bit by bit

The thunder starts to rumble its song
I know now it won't be very long
Before the power of the lightning starts to seethe
As the wind and hail gather speed

I feel the storm gathering against my window pane
I know I love it although it sounds insane
The bursting flashes of light and thunderous booms
Fills each and every one of my empty rooms

I sit and admire the brilliance of nature's forces
The storm arrives like thundering horses
Oh how the sky lights up with fire and light
So lucky am I to enjoy this wondrous sight

Don't Go There

The river is rising and the people are concerned
This has happened before the elders have learned
Not to wait till the river crests and floods all
As the houses are washed into the deluge they fall

The love of this land makes them all return here
But each time the floods come they know it's the year
That their hopes and their dreams can all be destroyed
Despite all their efforts and work that's employed

They live for the river high up on the bank
They know that location is the number one rank
But they ignore the fact that we all have to pay
When it comes down to it, this is no place to stay

The New Way

Water coursing out of the chasm
Washing away Humanity's old sarcasm
Melting away the hypocrisies and lies
Capitalism where everyone sells and buys

The illusion is so hard to see
But it is not best for you and me
Let's recognize the disguise of corrupt powers
But find they are protected as corporate towers

Tyrannies of laws and of human control
Who need the police and the border patrol
To keep us from taking responsibility for ourselves
That place is in our heart where our soul dwells

Trust in human nature I don't know
But we have to start somewhere however slow
Let's join up and make this system work
Instead of being just stuck in a quirk

Life

Candles in the dark are burning bright
Flames a flickering erratic light
Time is melting so quickly away
All we know is we have today

Searching for the eternal truth
Sometime we learn from the very uncouth
With struggles we learn the ropes of life
Regardless of the inevitable strife

We carry on our dancing waltz
And learn to accept all of our faults
Yet try to work to straighten them out
And we'll find what we are all about

Watch the candle wave in the breeze
A candle can never ever freeze
And the same bright light is within our souls
Fill each day with worthwhile goals

The Horse
(To My Four Legged Friends)

I am a fine lined Arabian mare
I love how the wind blows through my hair
I gallop in stride with the air in my face
I wish I could always keep up this pace

But I get tired and have to walk
If I see a friend i stop to talk
We all have many thoughts to share
Especially since I'm a wise young mare

My riders are many and come from afar
To get to my stable they drive in a car
Cars are frightening to me and so loud
They hurt my big ears with which I'm endowed

I want to gallop as fast as I can
My hooves thunder on the track that I span
Long distances are where I love to let go
But at some point I have to relax and walk slow

I am a flaming mare with a great mane and tail
When you ride me I stay right on the rail
My muscles are hard with the strength that I bare
My species are dwindling but does anyone care

You can ride me as I am sweet and I'm tame
I wonder if you can guess what is my name
I keep it a secret for only the few
And this secret is known only to you

Please keep me fed and give me some drink
And exercise me out in the big oval rink
Let me run free in the pastures out there
And you will be proud when my nostrils flare

Love me with kindness and tender care
And I will be with you as long as you're there
My name is a secret but remember my words
And you may just see me gallop free with the herds

Questions
(To Our Universe)

Time and consequence have personal meaning
Limited by our capacity to know
Our experiences shall be proven extremely limited
Our senses are made for survival alone

But we still are searching for the answers
To life's most plaguing questions
Those mysteries you want to understand
But just can't quite grasp with the human mind

Time Waits for None
(To Life)

Experience the fleeting perception of time
All can be changed by dreaming sublime
Face to face we meet our true selves
Instead of hiding on the shelves

Change is like climbing way up a rope
Transforming your cries into a song of hope
Just imagine what you can really do
And see it as something for you to pursue

Time waits for none of us
It's kind of like missing the bus
Our moments on earth are gone so fast
So it's time to make your life a blast

I Am a Tree
(To the Forest)

I am a tall and sturdy red coastal cedar tree
I can gaze over the tops of the alders and see
The Douglas firs compete with my great height
We struggle to get the best scenic sight

I am tall and straight and my bark so smooth
I swing with the breeze, in the wind I groove
My fronds sway in the wind as I sing my creaking songs
I am old and know all about history's right and wrongs

I stand tall in the park, safe here in the preserved
I get to be one of the few that gets to be reserved
My brothers and sisters are cut down by cruel men
When they are all gone, what the heck then….

Left alone in my park with my fellow survivors
A natural heaven on earth for my tree advisors
As I am still young considering some of these giants
And I depend on my safety from their reliance

Please admire my stature and grace
For I am living here with you in this place
We are really all one and the same
We just go by a different form and name

For my survival this is no game
Tree cutters far off causing such pain
I hope I will be saved here in this loving space
And not be part of the booming construction race

Pray for me and come visit me soon
I particularly like the sun at noon
I will show you my courage amidst the storm
And then you will understand why I was born

The Songs of Reality
(To a Different Tune)

From the years we begin with
We sing the eternal song
Even if cages surround us
We keep on singing
The same old song

But songs abound
And leap to be heard
All we have to do is listen
For that paradigm shifting lyric
That changes our world

And then we break free
With a new song
Those cages cannot trap

The Present

Can't you feel the powers of now
Present is already gone
The past is forever a memory
To do with as you will

Now is the mystery,
When does it start and stop
It's so quick
Live for the now
Those words can't define
Reserved for perceptual
Senses of beingness

We are consciousness that flows
From one moment to the next
We are moving through time capsules
Conscious of making every second count

So do what we choose, even if we stall
Carry on the mission to live for the now
And making the best use of it
This is your present

The Mission

We used to pray
But the outcome was gray
So we left that prayer
And studied ancient scripts

Many ways of expressing reason
But seeking something that transcends
Comforting that explains the cycle
I gasp to understand my mission

Those times were training grounds
The horror of fear
But now I understand
Where you are coming from

You may find me wrong
As I am not pretense
I'm a genuine animal of this human….race
I'm really part of you

The Migration
(The Birds That Survive the Journey)

Flapping feathers brushing the air
With wings so strong and delicate
They fly across the continents
Across the sea they whip their wings
They swiftly sail as they traverse the breeze,

You hear their cries as they span the sky
So sweet in voices singing in unison
Following their navigator of all skies
Enduring the distance the vigor of life

Flapping their wings with each heart beat
The wind gives them breath at times
Allowing them to glide on its air currents
Symphonic wings beat in feathered flight

The rain is harsh but they keep speeding on
Through the misty canyons they travel far
Their destination is far from here
But they can see way beyond the miles

To find their resting place, they bravely prevail
Fighting exhaustion and hunger they persevere
They must struggle on as life embraces them
Carrying them to their land of Eden

An Inquiry
(To the Philosophers)

After all what is consciousness?
Is it a bunch of chemicals or is it a soul?
Can we figure out its essence and what we are?
Are we just flesh, bones?
Chemical and electronic brains
Luring us to believe we are souls graced by God?
What is afterlife, is it all in our minds
And do our minds create our reality now and after we die,
Can we choose heaven or hell based on our thoughts only?
It is such that we create our own realities forever
Here and after we leave this beautiful planet
Given to us to rejoice and thrive in,
Many of us have such primitive ways though
Which may be our living downfall
In the never ending drama
the fighting and hatred, where is the love?
For love is heaven and nothing else
Can we choose that and survive these times
Only we can never know till the time comes
So live your life with love and acts of kindness
And you will have a gift that raises your soul to heaven

The Book
(To Better Times)

I want to leave this stupid place
I feel like I just pace and pace
Like an animal in a steel wire cage
I'm let out only to go on stage

I'm tired of acting and being so fine
I can easily take what is only mine
I feel like an object of no worth or need
Like a book that someone has to read

It's a boring book and you rate its existence
And you always put up such a resistance
But you see me as nothing but an assignment
An object that looks like it's out of alignment

So you go and you try to forget about it
And you have the chance to take off and just sit
Then you leave the book behind in the dirt like it is
And try to forget about all that it is…
NOTHING

Love and Lost
(To All Who Dare to Love)

"Love, they say it's better to have loved and lost
than to have never loved at all"

Love is a force of nature's insistence
It is a thread that connects us to existence
It serves a purpose in evolution
The fittest survive it's a revolution

To love and have it unrequited
Pains the soul so excited
It hurts so much you want to die
And all the time, it's just a lie

Love can be so precious and pure
But how can one really be sure
That their gullible hearts won't be broken
While all is forever thereafter unspoken

To All Of My Friends Here

To all my friends here I love you so
I think of you wherever I go
You make my heart shine and glow
And my spirit and strength begin to flow

I thank you all for being my friends
L love you beyond where the earth finally ends
Love shines forever as time can't steal
The love for you I always feel

You are all a guiding light for me
I hope that you can really see
My love for you is stronger than steel
All of you are so meaningfully real

The Spirit That Got Remembered

Screams rolling out of insides deep within
Humiliation gaining its vicious edge
Carving out the portraits of an image
Chiseled into a concrete sculpture of rock

This stone has become hard and gray
It is stable and sturdy, yet weak and cracked
Winds come through the chasm of doom
Rising out of the darkness of the abyss

Tainted soul, physical sense erodes our image
Destroyed by the weight of crumbling granite
Crumbling in time burdened with the weight of sorrow
Eventually disappearing, down to dust in the ground

Covered forever in time and space it lays there
Never to be seen again by the populace
Its mighty message still lingers though
For this poem tells it all

Shall I?

Faces all closing in on me
So near and threatening i cannot see
I want to run I want to flee
I wish someone would let me be

They haunt me daily in my head
Like the sight of all my blood so red
I feel it coursing through my veins
I have lost control of the reins

I am bent on a bad feeling streak
I feel like i am just a freak
I need someone so much like you
To survive each day and make it thru

I see the badness in my head
And wish sometimes that i was dead
I'd never need anyone again at all
I'd just leap off the bridge and simply fall

No sadness, pain, no fear, no remorse
My mind would be dead beyond recourse
I'd feel nothing but I'd miss the trees
And miss the fall and all the leaves

Oh what to do in this state of disgrace
How in this world do I keep up face?
I am so childish stupid and dumb
I just want to run and run and run

Away from myself as fast as I can
I'm nothing but a garbage can
Just put me out of misery
Erase my sense of history

The Trees and the Forest
(To Nature)

The trees whisper softly long songs of grace
They are not part of the human race
They stand so tall and stately proud
Above all this, they are never loud
They sway in the winds of ancient time
The trees are mysterious and sublime
They speak to us but can we hear
Other creatures can, they have the ear
We may miss the sounds, but see the sights
The forest bathes us in shimmering lights
Silver rays of sun, light the mist of the fog
Below on dense floor is an ancient log
The green in this place is so intense
And it holds a special fragrant essence
The deer peer at us with no fear in their eyes
They know that we carry no real lies
Sun light on dripping branches, dew drops are still
Each drop a shining light bulb, oh what a thrill
The sun makes its way across the sky
And as it does we wonder why
We live in a universe of reality that rolls
Our own reality that springs from our souls
Can our souls create our universe?
Or are we just on a fated life course?

Where and Why

Miles stretch out in waves always before me
As I travel in my craft ever so quickly
My final destination is not really clear
On my unwritten journey, I try not to fear

I look forward, not behind me
The future's path I strain to see
Traveling along lost, I'm not worry free
This path of mine is written upon the deep sea

I come round a bend and encounter a turn
Which way do I take, as I suddenly squirm?
I look both directions, which course do I chose
The choice is mine, but I don't want to lose

But the journey isn't written until the truth comes out
I'll find my destination as I ramble about
In my journey I fear each turn and each route
I look for some solace and courage from doubt

The unknown is the answer to all of our whys
The thought brings tears that run from my eyes
You can adventure along and take personal risk
Your future is not written on a CD-ROM disk

Travel to the Stars
(To the Universe)

The sun and sky are very high
To reach them both you have to fly
But they are unreachable you know
Unless in a special craft you go

There must be a shield that's solar and heat proof
Otherwise the sun would melt the roof
And you would be hotter than you ever have been
And the sun would be brighter than you've ever seen

I want to travel to the stars
I wish I could go and land on mars
But I'm here on this earth and happy with that
I just go on out and stand up to bat

The earth is a precious globe in space
It holds every animal and human race
It should be treasured each day and each night
From outer space it's gleam is a wondrous sight

Will the Forest Survive?
(To Earth)

High in the thin air of the mountain peaks
Trees sing songs of wind, movement and peace
Together they dance like waves in space
Creaky and swishing, they sway in pace

Below, kicking up their heels with joy
Donkeys play in the fields oh boy!
Romping just like young ponies do
Freedom their essence in morning's dew

The beauty of nature is hard to behold
Something that can't be bought and sold
We must preserve our wildlife and lands
From the stingy greed of humans' hands

Loss of Innocence
(To the Abused Children)

Many faces in a crowd
All screaming out aloud
Many times they have cried
Many times they have died
They feel so alone inside

They sit in the corner shedding tears
They hover shaking from their fears
Experiencing wrong o'er the eons of time
So afraid to step out of line

They are her and all of her selves
For long hiding on these shelves
Waiting vigilantly from inside her lair
Wondering if anyone will ever care

Lost at Sea
(To Dolphins)

I am alone on this voyage this sad lonely time,
I fell off the ship and am not in rhyme
Separated from crew members, my faithful friends
I wonder if I'll descend to bitter deep ends

I float on some wood that had drifted by
I lay on it as I silently cry
Where are my mates and where can I go
The shark fins are pointed, beginning to show

I climb onto my boat of wood and of tree
I wonder if I will survive this to see
To smell the salt of the deep ocean wind
I wonder if I'll be eaten, chewed up, and skinned

The sharks hover closer, their fins shining bright
I can see them gliding in the glimmering light
They come in much closer and bump on my raft
I may not survive on this flimsy wooden craft

But all of a sudden the sharks turn around
I hear in the distance a splashing sound
It's dolphins approaching my feeble float
They arrive in hoards and make a big moat

The sharks slink away and do not return
The dolphins teach me how to make the right turn
I swivel around and start following them fast
They go so darn quickly I hope I can last

But soon I see my ship and my mates
I wonder about all our separate fates
They pull me aboard and out of the sea
They are so happy to have rescued me

But the credit goes to the sea creatures so dear
They stay round a bit as I shed them a tear
I thank them for helping me find home and survive
And allowing me the chance to stay alive

Human Wrongs
(To the Forest and Creatures)

The forest has many unusual creatures and life
It protects them with shelter away from all strife
But sometimes there are forces beyond their control
And a carpet of danger starts to unroll

A fire can cause such havoc and fear
They run from it quickly the elk and the deer
But fire surrounds them in a flaming embrace
They cannot escape from this explosive place

This sad truth is seen every summer such loss
Death makes its rounds after one cigarette toss
It is humans who cause this death and destruction
Just learn ash tray cigarette disposal instruction

I am saddened by the ignorance and loss
All it takes is one quick careless toss
And the forest is burning raging bright
The chances for survival are very slight

Who am I?
(To Those Who are Lost)

I don't know who I am anymore
I have no idea what's possibly in store
I feel nothing existing in empty spaces
I see nothing but masquerading faces

I do feel pain of loss and despair
I feel like I'm beyond life's repair
I just stand at the window I look and stare
Everything just looks so very bare

Face yourself and silently scream
To me it's reality not just a bad dream
Grovel at the feet of fate
But never will this fear abate

The Forest Fire
(To Nature)

The animals in the forest run
For there appears an unnatural sun
It's flaming bright and hot as hell
It courses through in bursts that swell

Can the little ones escape this wrath of fire
They try to run but the small ones tire
To find water is their goal right now
In the heat of fire nature can't allow

The fire is consuming the forest fast
How much longer will these creatures last?
Can they escape the burning maze of flames?
As nature's forces' fury brazenly reigns

The animals fear that they will die
The forest is filled with a unison cry
They are on the verge of death
This may be their life's last breath

And no one can stop the torrent of heat
It looks like the creatures have been beat
They wait to feel the awful pain
When suddenly it starts to rain

Greed

Rules to obey every day
Everyone knows it's the way
They make us civilized, some contrive
Every day a new rule comes alive
Social norms are the blight to our fate
What happens when we arrive too late
Wrong is really one person's vantage
Thinking twisted to fit the advantaged

Must we bend to the rules,
Like sheep and end up at the fence
Many rules are driven by greed
And intemperance

Making no exceptions for those in need
This is the meaning of what I call greed

The Sun and the Sand

Glimmering sunlight sparkles on the water's smooth surface
The beach and the ocean are never superfluous
The gulls fly about and sing sea gulls' song
In this place of paradise nothing can go wrong

A magic scene of sand and bright sea
This place just exists, can anyone see
It glows like a beacon of hope when it's dark
And no in this ocean there isn't a shark

Please join me here, relax in the dunes
We will listen to earth's many fine tunes
You are all welcome to be here with me
To have some fun and dance round in glee

The Past
(To all who have suffered and continue to suffer from their past)

Today I am new but strangely old
There are many stories I have yet to have told
I feel so young and like a child
My heart and my head are spinning wild

I have no sense of who I am
All I know is I'm stuck in quicksand
I'm struggling hard to get myself out
But strength and courage I'm without

The past is my torment and destiny
Consuming every part of me
It invades my mind, my heart and soul
And in the end it takes its toll

I know that it's crazy, but I know it's true
I have the knowledge of how this all grew
I try to be present in this moment of time
I try to stand up and I try not to whine

A person should exist in reality's space
But I am a stranger to all in this place
I walk around blindly in a big gloomy fog
And as I can't see I get lost in a bog

My past intercepts me and beats me down
I feel that I will eventually drown
In this horrible past time, can I ever be fine
I am of no essence; I'm lost in a crime

Reverted to some place I hate to be in
I am starving myself I am now so thin
Just to hide away from all of this pain
Yet I feel l am going slowly insane

I am so scared I can't keep this up
I feel like a storm cloud about to erupt
I have such a problem with getting it right
I persevere and strive to keep up the fight

Wrong

Life is like the dark side of the moon
Pitch black no sun at all not anytime soon
I feel like I want to die i feel so dismal and discouraged
All I ever wanted from you was to feel encouraged

All I do is ask for support from your voice
But it's like you have no bloody choice
But to distain me at those critical times
You can't possibly read between the lines

I can't see the light anymore
I can't even see an open door
All the time that I've felt close to you
Is a sham because of what you do

You are hardened, I see through you
I have tested you and know it's true
It's like you can't understand me at all
I won't let you create my fall

I must beware of you
I don't now what to do
I have had a bond with you
But it's slowly becoming gone, it's through

You have said too much to hurt me so
Each time you have dealt me a fatal blow
And you smile and laugh about it
And you expect me to take every hit

In stride you are right according to you
I am wrong every time I can't win, never do
I am the fool, the loser in this game
Watch it because you are creating the same

Thing I most abhor about people…their arrogance
Their self righteousness and their rigid stance
I believe in caring and love
But for you this is something way above

I hate to see such ignorance
But that's what i see by your rigid stance
So be it I will have to think about this more
And decide if I can handle what else you have in store

The Lost
(To All Who Suffer)

I feel like I'm going insane inside
It's something that i must abide
But it's very hard to carry on
I no longer have a positive song
Because there is something really wrong

I am so anxious every day
It's like my brain is carried away
I can't control it at all
I am just about to deeply fall

I am screaming deep inside
I have no place to hide
I am a mess upon this place
I have no comfortable safer space

I am in trouble in a big way
That's all that I can really say
I can only help myself
But I'm stuck upon this shelf

I hate this feeling I want to scream
I wish it was just a silly dream
I struggle just to maintain my day
And to keep myself searching even if I have to stray

Another Storm Story
(To Life)

The storm rides high on the agitated ocean
The little boat rocks violently in the tumultuous motion
Lightening bolts crash thunderously down
The sailor fears now that he might just drown

The wind is howling fiercely, coursing the sea
The boat won't survive with out a huge fee
A debt to the gods to make him survive
And to watch over him and keep him alive

But what does he have to pay up these gods
And without them what are his odds
He is alone on his own in this vast tempest
He is so tired and weary he just has to rest

His boat is crashing against the waves
He is so tired and cold his soul can't be saved
He lets himself go as the boat cracks in two
And he silently sinks down into the deep ocean blue

The Other Storm
(To Everyone)

The sky is black with turbulent clouds
And the wind makes the trees bend and bow
The atmosphere is dense with negative ions
The storm is approaching like a bunch of wild lions

It has such great force and magnitude
It covers many a latitude
It is stronger than the people imagine
This storm sweeps in with a horrible raging

The birds are caught unawares
They try to dive away in pairs
But are swept into the hard dirt ground
Never again to chirp a sound

The storm has its vengeance upon the earth
It will die in time but have rebirth
To lay havoc upon the land once more
The creatures know what is in store

But meanwhile the devastation is clear
As the storm itself has no fear
It strikes at a whim and kills its prey
Its power is catastrophic in every way

Time

Time, a clock ticking steadily
Seconds, minutes pass so readily
Is it too late for me already?

My life is just a time clock
As I watch it in a stunned shock
Each moment goes by, tick by tock

My story is written in the past
And time is running much too fast
I fear for me, time won't last

Sleeping each night, waking each day
Time is life, a moment in a play
Oh my God, I just want it to stay

But it runs away so fast with me
Much more quickly than I can see
Oh I'm so afraid of what may be

The Children
(To all children who are misunderstood)

No flowers in this promised land
Only weeds that sting the delicate hand
This is a place of desolate things
Not even a bird chirps or sings

Barren landscape with tumble weeds
Any color in the sky recedes
It's dark and dusty with wind and sand
This is the children's destined land

They try to hover from the wind
Wondering if they have really sinned
They live in guilt and total shame
They think they are the ones to blame

No one can ever save them now
No one can really ever know how
Yes people just think they know what to do
But the children know they have no clue

Nature's Wrath
(To all who have died)

Waves crash against the sandy shore
The tide rushes in with the force of four
A storm is gathering deep in the sea
The seagulls decide they need to flee

Distant thunder is heard on the small island
The animals all skirt across the sand
This storm is black with reflections of green
It's the biggest one the people have seen

As it approaches the tide bursts on shore
Smacking the sand like never before
The swell of the water covers the sand
And soon it rises up and covers more land

The people flee their little homes of course
As the storm rages in and increases its force
Some are caught quite unaware
They didn't notice it enough to beware

They drown in the huge tide of water that heaves
Huge gallons of water before it recedes
And as it comes inland once more to kill
The sounds of screams are stark and shrill

The storm ends life as quickly as it comes
It wipes out life with watery runs
Over and over it strikes the island
And there is no one to lend a hand

The life of the world is so delicate and rare
It's hard to see the suffering as fair
But that's the way it has to be
In the forces of nature upon the sea

Hidden
(To those who must hide)

Screams rolling out of insides deep within
Humiliation gaining its vicious edge
Slicing the portraits of an image
Condensing into a concrete pillar

Stone become hard and gray
It is stable and sturdy yet weak and cracked
Winds come thru the chasm of doom
Rising out of the darkness the snake

Tainted soul and physical sense
Destroyed but trying to be like stone
Cracking in time with such weight
Crumbling down to dust in the ground

Bent iron and metal twist and cut hands
Blood runs down and pools in a mirror
To look at one's blood is perception
And the ground suddenly turns black

Island of Mine
(To the sun)

The sun shines today over the land
I walk on the beach my toes in the sand
The waves crash in and roll over my feet
The sun is a source of light and of heat

Sky of blue with streaks of white
Water so shiny, shimmering bright
Sand so warm and golden in hue
Sea water in sun reflecting deep blue

The tall graceful palm trees
Blow their fronds in the breeze
Seagulls cry cheerily in the sunlit shine
The sun is such solace on this island of mine

The Tree
(To the Cedar)

Trees are strong and free
That's how I want to be
I yearn for the red cedar wood
To reveal such beauty, if only I could

But I am a sapling blown in the wind
I wonder if I'll ever be able to bend
Not snap like a twig on a brittle end
Falling down to earth in a drastic descent

I am a tree, I am a plant
I am not human just a transplant
I blow in the wind and feel I'm not suited
Otherwise I would stand tall and be strongly rooted
I would be flexible, willowy and strong
And have a sense that I do belong

War Part 1
(To the Human Race)

War is a violent thing
When all the soldiers feel the sting
Of blood on their hands and bleeding cuts
An open door just suddenly shuts

The world becomes a place of fear
Where you find death so very near
It's not nature's way it simply seems
It's politics and greed, by every means

The poor ones die a horrible death
As they gasp for each last wheezing breath
They wonder what this was all about
As their life force slowly flows right out

This thing called war has gone on so long
And just in my mind it seems so wrong
Killing each other over territory and oil
It's enough to make my blood just boil

War 2
(To the Innocents)

The wars of different clans
The blood on all their hands
It's all because of an illusion
A major human delusion

Life can be so full of raw hatred
And the forces go out unabated
Of what they think is an intrusion
And the group mentality of exclusion

War is such human nature to some
They wait for the battles to overcome
Their enemies and foes they fight so hard
Spilling a pound of blood to advance one yard

But nobody really wins in the end
Because it all starts up again and again
War is so futile and cruel to life
It's just an example of human's great strife

War 3
To the Soldiers

The wind carries forth a message of truth
As it whips up in gusts and tears at the roof
The death of the soldiers was not of a need
So unneccessary it was that they had to bleed

I look to the wind to give me the word
Or how to explain what has just occurred
I can't quite hear clearly to get the full story
But it has to do with some men and their glory

Life is like magic a gift from above
This world should be more about caring and love
I will do my own part to cherish this place
And make it a walk instead of a race

Dragons

Dragons dragons of the night
Take off in their immortal flight
Swooping down to snatch their prey
They prey on me each and every day

Breathing out their streaming flames of fire
They drop their victims down into the mire
And return to the sky in search for more
All the innocents don't know what's in store

The dragons are here in my heart
They literally tear me completely apart
I fight them with my sword of strength
To banish them I'll go to any length

But to die from them is what I fear
They are after me and always near
They cover me with their flames of pain
And make me feel like I'm insane

They live in my world of darkness and woe
I want to destroy them and overthrow
Their venomous power and brandishing teeth
Snarling at me from above and beneath

I fight hard and bravely but it's clear
I feel it's a losing battle here
As the dragon's claws draw so very near
I tremble alone here shaking with fear

I draw my sword but it breaks in half
I start to run but there is no path
In darkness I blindly seek a way
But with me the dragons are here to stay

The Candle

A candle flickers in the darkness of a hot humid night
It shines like the afterburn of fading sunlight
A flame alone, created by a sad soul
Allowing her to see through its faint lonely glow

But darkness descends upon her head and her heart
It pervades her, her soul and saps her small spark
She feels the fear coming in a rushing motion
As she attempts to squelch all of her emotion

Only her and her candle, it burns for her sight
But soon she knows it will consume all its light
And all will descend into darkness and gloom
As the monsters appear against the misty moon

Run as she may it's her all alone
The monsters take presence and begin their roam
Inside her poor body, her spirit, her mind
With no candle beside her she's totally blind

The Loss
(To a Friend)

Rain beats against my window pane
I know all about you, your grief and your pain
As thoughts of you wander across my mind
Oh comfort and solace I wish you will find

As fall approaches the leave flutter down
They gather in piles of yellow and brown
As I look closely, it has yet to be found
The reasons for life and death, as the cycles rebound

Water soaks windows streaking the glass
Rain soaks the dirt and strands of the grass
Tears from the dark sky pour down on the earth
I ponder upon nature's death and rebirth

To give and to share our selves and our love
Must be the true answer to the questions above
So I sit and I ponder upon you my dear friend
And I will love you beyond the inevitable end

Firefly
(To You)

The night is lit with fireflies
And the sound of wailing cries
The darkness is a gloomy scene
With sparks of fireflies in between

The little creatures bring me hope
They lighten my sky with blips of hope
But they come and go so rapidly
They lose their light so vapidly

I wish i was in light of day
Instead of this horrendous play
Night time is a time of fear
And I can't even shed a tear

It's brilliant how the day is bright
But when the sun sets it is night
And then the torture begins again
Just like the clouds just turn to rain

I am an animal stuck in a prison
The light I see looks like a prism
I see stars in my head in streaks so bright
But eventually I with them will fade from sight

The Star
(To the Sky)

Life is a falling star
It comes from afar
And lights up for a second and then it is gone
But its beauty is seen in a moment's sight
As the seconds pass by, it extinguishes its light

It travels from miles away in the sky
Only to fall to earth and to die
But it has its moment of shimmering glory
And contains in a second a whole life story

Does anyone know it, it's story of flight
Does anyone care that it shines so bright
It streams across the planet's thin air
But lonely it is, its story can't share

It is a great beauty and luminous streak
When everything in sight can seem so bleak
In a flash suddenly its appearance is known
It's so bright and electric and only a stone

I wonder upon nature's great gifts
And why they can be so perfect but swift
So quickly it passes each moment in time
And loses its brilliance and all of its shine

It is a great blessing we all have to know
And inside our hearts we can make ourselves glow
If only we look for the gifts right out there
We might find a twinkle that proves that we care

Leaves
(To the Trees)

The trees are losing their golden leaves
I pick them up on bended knees
To save them for my picture book
Each one I take a closer look

To find a perfect leaf on the ground
Each one is a treasure I have found
I thank the nature god of trees
And choose each one just as I please

I find a red one perfect shape and size
A maple leaf I realize
It's just dropped off the tree above
And I treasure it with all my love

Each leaf is precious in its own way
I look at leaves change every day
And wonder if they just might feel sad
That they have fallen or are they glad

Life and Death
(To Life)

Rocky coral on the seabed floor
Sandy seashells lie on the ocean's shore
Gray and white clouds hover roiling above the tide
Seagulls cry out and the pelicans dive
The wind starts to swell as the waves tumble near
The boat heaves unsteadily and is difficult to steer
The rain starts to fall, distant thunder is heard
All go to shelter except for one bird
He doesn't realize that the storm thrashes near
The lightening and thunder now start to appear
The little lone bird is caught unawares
As the man in the boat just hangs on and stares
He watches in horror as the storm take its prey
Torn from the sky, the bird falls away
He drops in the sea, with a sad lonely sound
And never again will his life be around
The boat is rocking and fighting the wave
As the man holds the rudder against the storm's rage
He hits a high crest that breaks his boat's bow
And he sinks slowly downwards as death will allow

Alaska
(To the Wild)

The red and orange vibrantly radiate out their hue
Colors pervade the mountains advancing to the sky of blue
It's a sight to behold this color scheme of nature's appeal
It's hard to believe that this is all real

The mist covers the tops of this heavenly show
The colors reach a certain height and then turn to snow
White on red and yellow what a dream
And down below flows a cold shimmering stream

The land is carved out in the middle of the mountains
The waterfalls course down like graceful fountains
The air is so clean and pure it sings with the breeze
And close to this place are the glacier filled seas

The white snow rests so silently on the trees
This sight simply brings me down to my knees
It's a picture in my memories now but always mine
And I know after seeing this I'll be just fine

The whales kick up their tails and roll with the sea
They frolic together in the deep blue with such glee
The seals sit on rocks shining coats in the bright sun
They look so peaceful with no need to run

This place is magical and wild
I look out in wonder with the eyes of a child
I want to keep these memories close by
As I watch eagles launch off limbs and swiftly fly

Sailors' Saga – Part One

We are on a ship headed way out to sea
We have no idea what the future might be
Our boat is quite sturdy but we feel such a fright
As we head out into deep water, with the land out of sight

But we sing this song as we pull up our sails
To help us survive our scary travails

"The sun shines out upon the land
We gather together and each joins a hand
It's a day of light and joy and being ness
It's a time of joining hands and oneness
The warmth of the sun seeps into our skin
We have what it takes to allow us to win"

But as it grows dark we feel so afraid
We cry out what to do as we enter the shade
We tremble as we remember past trips we have made
Suffering endured in our souls, such degrade

So we sing out this song to give us some power
And sing it out loud we sing for an hour

"We seek comfort from life that surrounds this great ark
Our courage shines out through the encroaching night's dark
We all are one and need love and some kindness
Instead of hate and cruelty and blindness
We stand up for peace and love and what's right
And we have already won the fight"

The sea gets unsteady and a storm approaches near
This is the time when we begin to feel fear
The wind whips our sails, waves crash on our ship
The rain falls down hard and we start to lose grip

We must hang on tight to brave out this storm
But all of a sudden the sail becomes torn
We all gather together even though we are worn
And seek solace together from the cold and forlorn

We feel so weak and cold in our bodies and minds
But remember our resources, all sorts and all kinds
But for now all we can do is hang onto the ship
And pray that no one comes loose with one slip

And we sing out our next stormy sea song
To make us have courage and to make us feel strong

"This night is a storm
But we are not torn
We have what it takes
To manage the stakes"

And as the storm dies and the morning comes through
We sew up the sails and make them look new
We have lots of hands and our team on our side
So we take these hardships and resolve them in stride

But fear is upon us for we are so new
We don't know whether our courage is really true
We seek out enlightenment from the heavens above
And as we do we glimpse a white dove

We follow its flight to lead us to land
And with luck we finally see the gleaming white sand
It's there in front of us like a shimmering light
And we know that this trip was a wondrous flight

The Raging Storm – Part Two

Standing near the ocean's shore
The crew knows already what's in store
This will be a dangerous trip
And one where all may lose their grip

But they tell each other that it will be fine
Each one knows he or she must tow the line
Well they set off amidst a raging torrent
All feel the fear oh so abhorrent

But they sing a new song
And they sing it along
With the music of the thunder
And their fear they of being pulled down under

"Our mighty ship is sturdy and strong
We must not fear, our hearts will sing out this song
The sea will hold us up like a handful of cotton
And we know we will never be swept to the bottom"

And as they emerge from the frightful storm
They realize that their bow has been terribly worn
So they struggle to fix their mighty vessel of wood
They cry out in pain with their sweat and their blood

And as they toil they sing out a tune
While they search the sky for a guiding moon

"No our effort is not in vain
It is worth all of this terrible pain
We can save our life boat swaying here
And we know that the angels are always near"

They finally mend their broken boat
And as they do, once again it begins to float
Back on their journey to the deep they go
Behold! Stars fall from the sky, an exploding light show

And they watch the stars with tears in their eyes
As they see the stark beauty of the starlit skies
And what they could have potentially lost
If their ship had been destroyed and unforgivably tossed

And each one prays to the shining stars
To help them rid them of their scars
For they have been so badly beaten and maimed
While all the time they were being blamed

Their hearts sing a song
For it has been long

"Our hearts are so sad
But we can make them become glad
For the stars shine out so bright
And this is our starlight night"

And they journey along to the next ordeal
And have no idea of what they will feel
But they stand together as a sibling crew
And know each day will bring something new….

Sailors' Saga – Part Three

The sailors continue along their way
They wish for an island to dock on and stay
Just for a rest for they are so weary
They are so weak and their eyes are bleary

They scan for a shore to rest their tired souls
They are worn from their demanding sailor's roles
When suddenly they spy a land mass of sand
And it looks like a place where they can land

So they set off for the island with hope in their hearts
And pray there's no danger like man eating sharks
But they need to rest so off they go
And sail to the island to make it so

They land in the sand which is a brilliant white
They secure their great boat with ropes all tight
And they walk towards the trees that line the beach
And look for water that may be within reach

But suddenly they are surrounded by tall strange creatures
They don't look like people but have similar features
They have four legs but the face of a person
They look like centaurs but a different version

The crew feels quite afraid of this unusual sight
And wonder how they can escape this fearful plight
The creatures start coming closer in fast
The crew fears that their time on this earth is now past

The creatures surround them making very strange sounds
The crew thinks they surely have stepped out of bounds
They sit down in fear and hold each other tightly
They don't take their closeness in anyway lightly

The creatures come closer to look at the crew
The sailors feel like they are finally through
But the creatures began singing the crews' sea faring song
And the crew soon realizes they will all get along

The creature has special sensory perceptions
And they can read the crews' minds and all their conceptions
This is strange to the crew and a bit unnerving
But the creatures make them feel very safe and deserving

They get to know each other quite nicely and fast
And all make a friendship that surely will last
They eat a great meal and dance round the fire
until each one is exhausted and begins to tire

They all fall asleep into a deep, deep slumber
And dream about their trips and the distant thunder
They awake in the morning and the creatures are gone
But far in the distance they see a small fawn

It stares at them with sad, glistening eyes
The look on its face brings about the crew's cries
She looks so sad and lost in her way
The crew starts to sing a song and to pray

The little fawn approaches them slowly with fears
They bring her some food and wipe away all her tears
They decide to adopt her and take her on their ways
As they tell the little fawn she dances and plays

So with new supplies and water aboard
They set off again to search out the ocean's accord
And the fawn is so happy to have found such new friends
And is free to be herself as there are no pretends

The crew and their new mate are back on the sea
And wonder what their next adventure might be

Sailors' Saga – Part Four

The crew realizes the fawn has been abused
Her inner soul has been used and bruised
She walks on 3 legs and can't stand up tall
Each step she takes looks just like she will fall

She has horrible wounds on her sides
The blood upon her slowly dries
She never sheds a tear and just hangs her head
And her nose drips blood that's a deep deep red

She is so weak from her destructive past
The crew wonders if she will last
They try to comfort her with care
But all she does is hide and stare

She remembers all of the venomous pain
The falling down in the pouring rain
Being kicked and beaten without a thought
She has been stolen, traded, broken, and bought

The little fawn is dying in our arms right here
She trembles at our touch as we try to hold her near
She won't look us in the eye
She says she really wants to die

We try to sing her our song of love
And we pray to our angels up above
But she seems so sad and so forlorn
Says she wishes she never was born

We also know this feeling too
It pierces our souls through and through
And we all fall to the boat's wooden floor
We feel we can take this pain no more

But a moon shines brightly upon our hearts
The ones that have been pierced with many darts
But the moon seems to heal our pain and sorrow
With its promise of the miracle of a tomorrow

But the little fawn's wounds don't seem to heal
Her damaged and beaten body is so real
She's been alone and abandoned all along
And she's never heard a seafaring song

So we try again to get her to live
And to her another song we give
She slowly lifts up her swollen fair head
And says that she wants to just be dead

But we help her by singing together along
Singing out our favorite and courageous song
And slowly she goes into a gentle sleep
As we continue to sail upon the deep

Ongoing Sea Saga – Part Five

The crew set sail for unknown waters
Knowing that kinship and strength matters
They sail along with caution and care
They are not in the mood to take on a dare

Suddenly cold water seeps into their craft
And behold they realize they have no raft
They know right now that they will surely drown
As their ship sinks further and further down

They jump off their home and hit the cold deep
And as they do, they begin to weep
They have lost their boat and now their life
Why they wonder must they face such strife

Alas! a strange creature glides towards them
A silver sea serpent with scales amen!
They cower together in a horrible fright
The serpent appears as a terrible sight

But low and behold it comes up with a smile
I have come to save you and take you awhile
On my back I will carry you safe and sound
Until some land can be searched out and found

The crew climbs aboard this unusual ride
They hold on tightly as they glide astride
The serpent swims gracefully through the sea
The crew are amazed at how this could be

Just then they see just out in the distance
Land ahoy and they ride without resistance
They reach the land and then disembark
Thanking their friend who has been their ark

They walk to the shore and lay down to rest
And know for now they must do their best
They will have to build a brand new ship
And do it right so nothing will slip

A new ship is their mission from this day on
So they rest their bodies and sing a song
And wait for the night to turn into day
For they plan to begin at light's first ray

The Childrens' Plight – Part Six

The sea is rough and full of danger
Each sailor feels just like a stranger
Somehow detached from the others now
Just wondering what to do and how

Some thing has happened to their bond
There's a pang of fear that's a wave beyond
Alone in each other's company they sigh
They feel separated and don't know why

Life is nothing but hatred and fear
They don't see a light or know of love here
They see blackness and gloom outside and inside
And they're aware that there is no place to hide

They hunger with realization, but still must abide
With all the terror that they each feel inside
Nothing can subdue the eternal nightmare
The long cold history that they each are aware

So they just lie down and cry wishing for dawn
With the sun they hope they will be less withdrawn
While in the meantime they just sob and cry
And hope that they won't just give up and die

When all of a sudden comes a glimmering red sun
And they look to the east from where it comes from
They stop their crying and set sail again
And set a new course to escape all their pain

Printed in the United States
59018LVS00006B/232-282